# FIRES IN THE WILD

## Contents

# FIRES IN THE WILD

Many fires in the wild are caused by humans, often by accident. Fires can get out of control by farmers burning off pastures to bring on new grass. Some campers light fires near dry leaf litter, which catches fire and spreads. A few fires are started by people who wish to make trouble.

...catches fire
**and spreads...**

# fan the flames

Fires in the wild can be caused by natural phenomena, too. For example, lightning may ignite dead grass, leaves, twigs, or bark (called litter) on a forest floor, then wind may fan the flames and drive them onto the bark, leaves, and branches of trees. Radiant heat from the fire dries out the green foliage, which will catch fire when the temperature is high enough.

Convective heat dries out the forest canopy – the branches overhead – and carries cinders up to them. The oil in the leaves of eucalypt and pine trees makes them burn fiercely.

## Clarify

### PHENOMENA

a criteria

b causes

c events

a, b, or c?

convective heat

**Complete the table.**

| CAUSE | EFFECT |
| --- | --- |
| lightning | ignites dead grass |
| wind | fans flames |
| convective heat | ? |
| oil in leaves | ? |

radiant heat

radiant heat

# How Fires Spread

## Predict

What do you think this chapter might tell us? How do you think fires might spread?

Forests have plenty of fuel and air, so fire spreads quickly and can destroy every living thing. Sometimes houses or whole towns are burned to the ground. Hot, dry summer days with strong winds are dangerous. If there have been heavy spring rains, there may be lots of new growth during summer to catch fire.

Fires in the wild can travel quickly, burning large areas of land. They can start in forests, grassland, and even in crops, like paddocks of wheat. These fires are dangerous to fight. The radiant heat from an advancing fire can kill people. The fire can burn up all the oxygen, causing firefighters to suffocate. Smoke can injure people's lungs and eyes. The fire can suddenly change direction and surround a town, leaving people no way to escape.

A fire in the wild will move ahead quickly if the litter is dry. In half an hour, several acres may be alight.

Forests have plenty
of fuel.

Hot, dry summer days
with strong winds are
dangerous.

# How Fires in the Wild Are Controlled

Fires in the wild are controlled by specially-trained firefighters who use a diverse range of fire-fighting strategies. Firefighters must work as a team. They must know how to survive a fire if it traps them.

Careful planning and good communication are vital. Some communities employ a full-time team leader to take charge during a fire. The leader may train the town's firefighters, and plan how to deal with future fires. Leaders must have up-to-date information about the fire, the weather, and the place where every member of the team is working.

Clarify

**DIVERSE**

*a* different
*b* alike
*c* separate

a, b, or c?

Firefighters **must** work as **a team.**

# FIRE-FIGHTING STRATEGIES

Fires in the wild can be stopped by using a variety of strategies.

## fuel

1. **Remove the fuel**, and the oxygen has nothing to react with. The fire dies.

## oxygen

2. **Remove the oxygen**, and the fuel molecules have nothing to react with. The fire dies.

3. **Remove the heat**, and the fuel cannot break down into active molecules. The fire dies.

**retardant**

4. **Add a retardant** to fire-fighting water, and the water will soak deeply into the fuel. The fire dies.

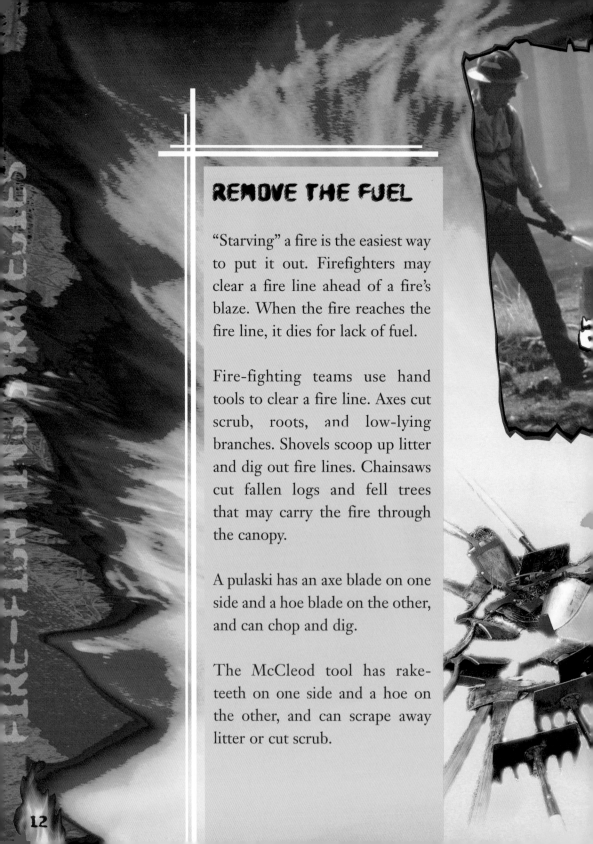

# REMOVE THE FUEL

"Starving" a fire is the easiest way to put it out. Firefighters may clear a fire line ahead of a fire's blaze. When the fire reaches the fire line, it dies for lack of fuel.

Fire-fighting teams use hand tools to clear a fire line. Axes cut scrub, roots, and low-lying branches. Shovels scoop up litter and dig out fire lines. Chainsaws cut fallen logs and fell trees that may carry the fire through the canopy.

A pulaski has an axe blade on one side and a hoe blade on the other, and can chop and dig.

The McCleod tool has rake-teeth on one side and a hoe on the other, and can scrape away litter or cut scrub.

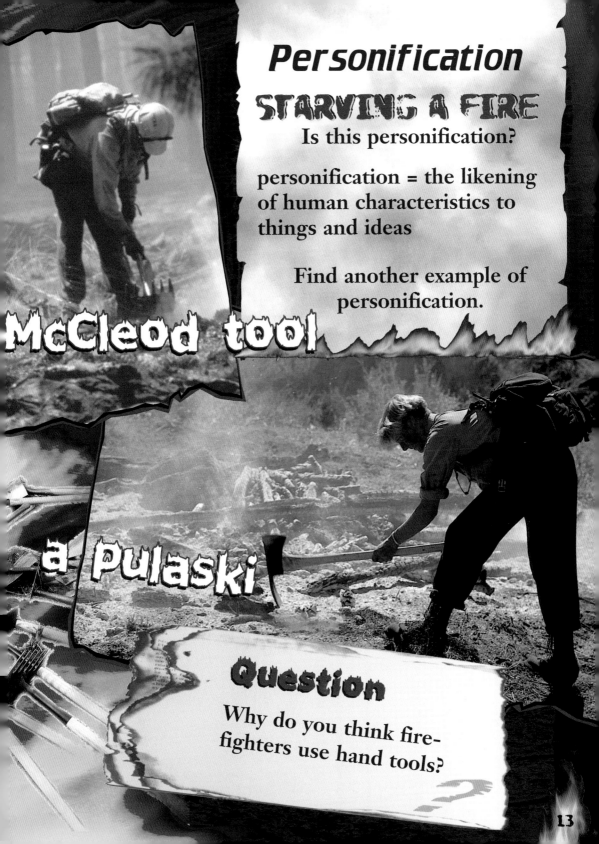

# Personification

## STARVING A FIRE

Is this personification?

personification = the likening of human characteristics to things and ideas

Find another example of personification.

McCleod tool

a Pulaski

## Question

Why do you think fire-fighters use hand tools?

Firefighters also starve a fire using a backburn, which is another fire lit ahead of a fire in the wild and carefully controlled. It creates a large area of land containing no fuel. When the fire reaches the backburned area, it will die and spread no further.

A backburn can be lit by a firefighter using a drip torch, or by dropping incendiaries from an aircraft.

# INCENDIARY

**a** a bomb designed to start a fire

**b** a match

**c** a parachute

**a, b, or c?**

# Light a backburn with a drip torch

## REMOVE THE OXYGEN

A simple way to remove oxygen is to smother the fire by beating it with a branch of green leaves, a wet sack, or a wet blanket. A fire can also be smothered by throwing sand or earth on it.

## REMOVE THE HEAT

A simple way to remove the heat from a fire is to smother it by throwing water on it. But fires in the wild often occur where there is little water, such as rocky, mountainous country. Fires usually begin in summertime, or during a drought.

Firefighters try to drive tanker trucks close to the fire. Their trucks have a pump that forces water from the tank through hoses. A portable pump can be used to refill the tanker from a nearby dam or river. If the fire is near a town, firefighters can refill the tanker from underground pipes with a hydrant.

Firefighters use hoses from a tanker truck to spray water on the fire. They can put out a burning fire or soak the fuel ahead of it. They also carry water on their backs in knapsack sprays to put out "spot" fires that have escaped from the main blaze.

fire

WORD ORIGIN
# HYDRANT
Where did this word come from?

Look in the dictionary.

...soak the fuel

ahead of the fire

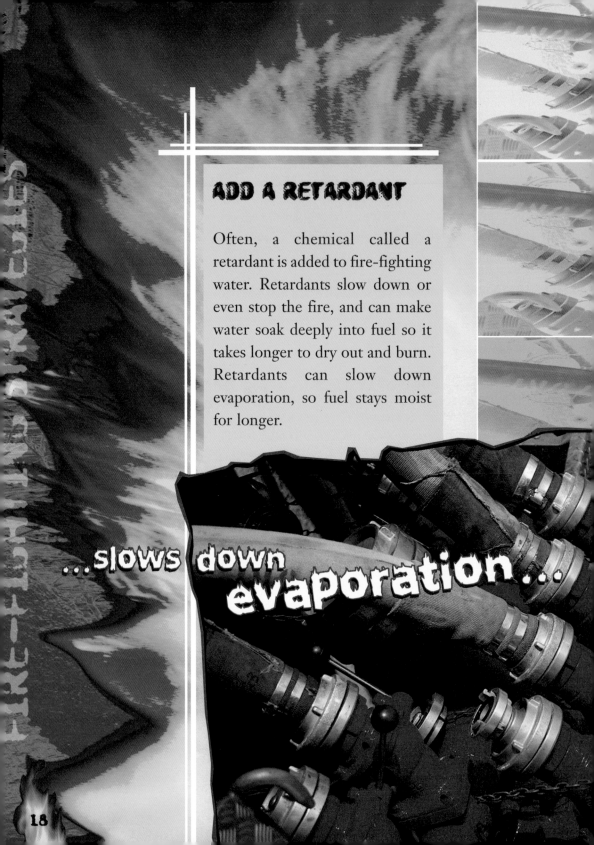

## ADD A RETARDANT

Often, a chemical called a retardant is added to fire-fighting water. Retardants slow down or even stop the fire, and can make water soak deeply into fuel so it takes longer to dry out and burn. Retardants can slow down evaporation, so fuel stays moist for longer.

...slows down evaporation...

## Complete the table.

# COMPARE AND CONTRAST
## the strategies of fire-fighting

| Remove the fuel | Remove the oxygen | Remove the heat | Add a retardant |
|---|---|---|---|
| **?** | beating with a branch of green leaves, wet sacks, or a wet blanket | **?** | add a retardant to fire-fighting water |

# How Fires in the Wild Are Fought from the Air

Aircraft such as fixed-wing air tankers and helicopters are used to fight fires from the air.

Air tankers are large aircraft that carry liquid tanks. They can drop thousands of gallons of retardant ahead of a fire. Some air tankers can refill by flying low over a lake and scooping up water. Air tankers can also drop equipment and supplies to firefighters.

## Question

What inferences can be made about the benefits of fighting fire from the air?

Air tankers can drop thousands of gallons of retardant ahead of a fire.

# HOW HELICOPTERS ARE USED

Helicopters can carry crews, supplies, and equipment quickly, land in paddocks, clearings, and other open areas close to a fire, attack fires themselves, or observe and report information to leaders.

A "helibucket" slung beneath a helicopter can dump buckets of water or retardant on a fire. The helibucket can also carry water to refill a tanker truck.

Helicopters are also used to carry specially-trained firefighters who rappel down ropes as the helicopter hovers overhead. They then fight the fire on the ground, or carry supplies and equipment to other firefighters.

rappelling down

a **helibucket** slung

**beneath**

a **helicopter**

## Clarify
# RAPPEL

*a* to descend a vertical drop by a rope

*b* to climb

*c* to drop

*a, b,* or *c?*

**ropes**

# HOW SMOKE JUMPERS HELP IN THE FIGHT FOR CONTROL

Smoke jumpers are firefighters who jump from aircraft, using a parachute to land. They are often the first to reach a fire in the wild.

Once they land, smoke jumpers attack the fire like other fire-fighters, cutting a fire line with hand tools.

Smoke jumpers must be very fit, and spend many months training. They must carry all their equipment and supplies for three days. When their work is done, they still have a long and weary hike ahead of them, to get back from the area.

cut a fire line with

smoke jumpers jump from aircraft...

hand tools...

# How Communities Are Alerted

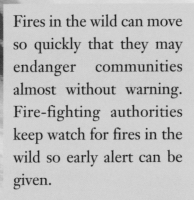

## Predict

**What do you think this chapter will be about?**

Fires in the wild can move so quickly that they may endanger communities almost without warning. Fire-fighting authorities keep watch for fires in the wild so early alert can be given.

Observers in lookout towers scan forests for smoke. They use a compass to find the exact direction of the smoke and radio this information to their headquarters.

The information from several towers is marked on a map, and the fire's exact location is found.

In many remote areas, automatic weather stations are set up. The stations send data such as temperature, humidity, and wind speed by radio, and this information allows firefighters to measure the fire danger. In many communities, large Fire Danger Meters are also set up to warn citizens about the risk of fire.

After a fire passes, forests will regrow, houses can be rebuilt, and towns may rise again, but the lives of people can never be recovered.

forest regrowing after a fire

# KEY POINTS

Select the key points you would incorporate in a summary.

- Fires in the wild are fought from the air.

- Sometimes houses or whole towns are burned to the ground.

- Fires in the wild can travel quickly.

- Fire-fighting authorities watch for fires in the wild so early warning can be given.

- Some communities employ fire-fighting leaders.

- Helicopters dump water on fires.

- Fires can be fought using a variety of strategies.

- Sometimes smoke jumpers are the first to reach fires in the wild.

- Fires begin in summer.

# Think about the text

Making connections — What connections can you make to the events and the human responses explored in *Fires in the Wild*?

behaving irresponsibly

communication

teamwork

**TEXT-TO-SELF**

leadership

cooperation

responding to danger

working under pressure

working in dangerous situations

# TEXT-TO-TEXT

Talk about other texts you may have read that have similar features. Compare the texts.

# TEXT-TO-WORLD

Talk about situations in the world that might connect to elements in the text.

# Planning an Informational Explanation

**1**  Select a topic that explains why something is the way it is or how something works.

**2**  Make a mind map of questions about the topic.

How are fires in the wild caused?

How do fires in the wild spread?

How are communities alerted?

## FIRES IN THE WILD

How can people stay safe?

How do smoke jumpers help in the fight for control?

How are fires in the wild fought from the air?

**3**  Locate the information you will need.

library          Internet          experts

**4** Organize your information **using the questions you selected as headings.**

**5** Make a plan.

Introduction

**Some fires in the wild are caused accidentally by humans, and others can be caused by natural phenomena.**

Arrange your points in a coherent and logical sequence.

| How fires in the wild spread | How fires in the wild are controlled | How fires in the wild are fought from the air | How air tankers and helicopters are used | How smoke jumpers help in the fight for control | How communities are alerted |
|---|---|---|---|---|---|

**6** Design some visuals to include in your report.

You can use graphs, diagrams, labels, charts, tables, cross-sections...

# An Informational Explanation

**A**  Explores causes and effects

**B**  Uses scientific and technical vocabulary

**C**  Uses the present tense

**D**  Is written in a formal style that is concise and accurate

**E**  Avoids author opinion